FINISHING LINE PRESS

www.finishinglinepress.com

Stepping Back

poems by

Barbara Roth

Finishing Line Press
Georgetown, Kentucky

Stepping Back

Publisher: Leah Maines

Editor: Christen Kincaid

Cover Art: Barbara Roth

Author Photo: Victor Roth

Cover Design: Elizabeth Maines

Printed in the USA on acid-free paper.
Order online: www.finishinglinepress.com
        also available on amazon.com

Author inquiries and mail orders:
Finishing Line Press
P. O. Box 1626
Georgetown, Kentucky 40324
U. S. A.

Table of Contents

To my mother who kept every scrap of paper on which I wrote a poem and my husband who encourages me to write and follow my dreams.

Writing

Paint the poems across the pages
Sing the melody into the night
never to be published
But sung until the moon fades in the morning
The words dance at the slightest thought
much like
chasing the shadows
  across the soybean fields yellowed by Autumn
Following the geese as they begin their Winter migration
And calling the dogs home for the night

Procrastination

Sometimes
  It is easier to let go
To deadhead the blooms from the roses and let them fall
  through my finger tips
To brush Bella, letting the morning breeze carry her soft hair
  to bushes
  where chickadees may gather the long strands for nests
Sometimes
  A good-bye is softer, gentler than a hello
It is a way of letting go, of packing memories to be opened later
  when there is time to appreciate what they were
Just as
Sometimes
  It is easier to give in to the day
Stepping over books, still to be read, shoes yet to be worn
To get my coffee, pet the cat
And go outside to discover what the rain has left in the garden
  overnight
And sometimes
  It is easier to listen
Letting the words flow around me as my own thoughts
  flit in and out
Just as
Sometimes
  It is easier to finish the book I am reading, the letter half written
Wash the dishes on the counter
So that I can begin again.

Beach Crows

They scatter
with raucous caws
soaring clouds of shiny black feathers
  dipping, teasing
  the early beach arrivals
Only to return later
  pulling towels off vacant chairs
  chasing seagulls in hopes they drop their cherished shells
Gangs of three
  digging chips out of unwatched picnic baskets
They rule the beach
Even the terns
  glide above their radar
  or move farther out to sea in search of food
With their sharp eyes and loud vocalization
I have seen the crows chase osprey until the fish is dropped
back into the dark waters
I think it is a game to them
They must keep score amongst themselves
  points given for each person, each bird they send into confusion
perhaps the repetitive caws that pierce the air
  are their version of laughter
As once again they have claimed the beach
And all others are in retreat

An Unfinished Morning

The morning excuse for rain
  has left behind air that is heavy, still
so dense even the ferns are not moving
The sky an unrelenting blanket of slate
  with no seagulls trailing on the horizon
Damp stuffiness permeates the woods
  and the chipmunks sprawl in false innocence across the patio

Not even a distant bark of a dog breaks the achingly somber silence
  of the day

The Neighbors

The porch sits empty now
  surrounded by pristine white railings
It looks lonely
  and the blue door too bright to be welcoming
I miss the mix matched rocking chairs
The chipped gray paint of the porch floor
  and the scratched oak door
I miss the laughter
that billowed out through open windows
  on a soft Spring night
The flash of Scout racing for the paper
  then begging for the quick toss of a tennis ball
I ache to hear the murmur of voices
  when friends dropped by
But another move, another change
And in so many ways the five miles down the road
may as well be ten

The Barred Owl

Pausing in the twilight
The sun's shadows through the trees
  long since faded
We step softly upon the crisp leaves
  and slippery moss of the woods
Finding
a silhouette pressed close to the birch
  feathers blending with the grays and whites of the bark
Then he turned his head
eyes unblinking to stare back at us
No motion, no other movement but those fathomless eyes
As he sat watching
guarding his young, yet to fledge
A gift of the quickly falling night

The Art of Life

Your watercolors lay scattered throughout the house
  remnants of a life yet to be finished
There, perched on the shelf
  one of Zoe, eyes already foggy with age
And below
  the house, drawn in crisp clear lines
Defining on paper
  boundaries yet to be crossed
Elsewhere, above the desk
  the waves swirl around rocks near the lighthouse
Rocks where we once sat on a late afternoon in July
  watching the sea ducks sail into the wind on those same waves
Not seen
  are the lines etched into your brow with each passing year
Or the paintings whose colors never touched paper
        but lived their life behind your eyes
        in the lost hours you sat contemplating the landscape
        before you
Letting the images swirl through your mind
But those you did capture with careful strokes of color to paper
Now rest front and center
        on walls, shelves, tables
A visual reminder of a moment before it became a memory

A Good Book

The words stretch across the paper
like a caterpillar inching its way through the grass
Holding my attention
just long enough
to wonder if the butterfly will emerge come Spring
Will the plot thicken
or an end become apparent too soon
Turning another page as one would follow a squirrel
his mouth full of leaves, hoping to see the nest
I am searching for reassurance
that the words have a journey
that I am not Alice missing the rabbit
to fly away to Neverland
and then, there it is
The turning point of heading home
staying up late
The author teasing me just enough
to keep the light on, the pages turning
Ah
The gift of a story well told

Memory of a Summer Day

I carry the blue sky with me
  on such days as this that are cold and dreary
Though March has arrived
  the snow and ice still cake the city sidewalks
Despite the birds waking me each morning
  with their courting songs
I see no signs of Spring to greet me on my morning walk
But I carry the blue sky with me
  on such days as this
I feel the warmth of the sun from that summer day
  caressing my weary body
I remember bending to pick the blossoms from my garden
  but hearing the bees as they buzzed and danced
  within the deep centers
  filling themselves with unseen nectar
  while hummingbirds hovered nearby
  their wings moving furiously, impatient for a turn to drink from
  the gift of the cosmos
  as it gently unfurled its glory
I stepped back
Choosing instead to pull out my palette
  and a delicate brush, fibers soft
But could not find a color to capture that flower
  as it lifted it coppery petals to the sky
letting the light enrich the glowing veins etched delicately
  amidst its beauty
  seeming to stretch taller toward the powder puff clouds
  floating in the cerulean sky
While I lingered in the peace of the moment

The Japanese Maple

The Japanese maple has surrendered to the rain
  after it courted her all night
First with gentle drops
  nourishing her dry, parched leaves
  whispering promises of more
As she bent and reached out from beneath the shade of the pine
  accepting this gentle attention
And as hours moved on
The wind picked up bringing heavier rain
to which she danced and trembled
  quaking in the joyful showers of affection
Now in late morning
  her branches worn from a night of flirtation
She turns her billowing red leaf skirt inside out
Displaying an intimate gentler contrast of color
A surrender to the orchestrated courtship of nature.

Song of LIfe

He tells stories
  woven from cobwebs of memory
  a tapestry framed in the wood scavenged from an old barn
While she sings songs
  on a guitar passed down from relatives
  living deep in the hills of the Blue Ridge Mountains
His stories dance across the flames of the fire late at night
While her voice cries with the ache of heartbreak
Prisms hung in windows
  keep rainbows alive in the cabin
While owls keep watch outside the windows
  on full moon nights
He dreams of settling down
  of a book on a shelf in a store
While she longs to bow to an audience
  on a stage with bright lights
And still
When dawn breaks
They pull the quilt closer
And he weaves his stories into her music
So their song can be sung

Fog

The fog swirls softly, lazily
  skimming the hillsides across the water
Then like a long cloak, begins to blanket the sandy beach
  that moments ago sparkled under the brief gift of sun
Slowly it stretches, shifting
  now the buoy is lost in its translucent web
soon the rocks below me are invisible
I am left
  with only the sound of the waves gently shifting, lapping at the beach
And the comfort of a single tall birch reaching for the sky

Zoe

Momentarily
  I am frozen, caught off guard
  my heart contracting with long buried aches
There, perched on the dresser
A photo
  She is standing, ready as always
  alert to the camera
  poised to play, tail high
You, next to her
  smile easy, tranquil
It was the perfect day
We had stopped along the rocks
  for what, I don't remember
  just that our hearts were light
I could not resist
  capturing the day with my camera
Now, three years later
The sight of the two of you
  forever in that moment
Tugs at my heart
And I close my eyes against this day
Listening with the hope of hearing her race up the stairs
  so that I may run my fingers through her long coat
One more time

Moving Day

She is folding her bag closed again
  nimble fingers
  a child of organized spaces
Even on this humid July afternoon
  carefully she tucks the ends of the bag around the crusts
  of her soggy peanut butter sandwich
Yet moments later
  she is found opening her bag
  and taking a bite from the same bedraggled meal
Once more folding the bag closed around those crusty ends
Whose child is this
None of us were ever so frugal
Sandwiches disappeared like June snowflakes whenever given to us
Fascinated, I watch her slow progress through this simple repast
Somehow she makes the sandwich last throughout the afternoon
  daintily wrapping and unwrapping it before each bite
While we shuttle boxes around her

Phone Call From Afar

Breathless, fresh from a morning walk
The sound of the phone
A voice from the past, hesitant, soft
Oh my friend
The year you have had
Your paintings bared to the soul
the anguish of losing your son
Yet hope is etched in the eyes of those you paint
   even as the very figures shrug deep within themselves
   holding candles, symbolic of hope
Of a life that lives on even though we can no longer hear the
 music he played
The vitality of his presence in a room
   the echo of his tread in the forest stays with us

Just hearing your voice
My own memories
Childhood
You with pigtail braids, the freckles
Nights of Wizard of Oz
   plays in the Carriage house
Cleo, kittens

How we grow
stretch through life
Your wedding, the aura of joy surrounding you and your love
Your daughter as an infant in New Hampshire
Blueberry pie and treasure hunts

Sitting on the porch in Pennsylvania
your rooster making paths around us
   while Rudy, your ever present Golden held him at bay

Always you are in my heart
Your spirit so gentle, touches many
Your friendship a gift through the years

Lost

Like out of season snowflakes
  drifting to brush the tops of early crocus
Your tears
  take me by surprise
your shaking sigh and soulful eyes
  shatter the tenuous hold I have on the day
Gazing through rain streaked windows at the leaf strewn yard
  my thoughts drift
    vignettes of moments shared flit aimlessly through my mind
Paths cobblestoned together
  somehow led to this moment of sadness that envelopes us
Perhaps it is not the day that is rain streaked but
My spirit that is tear torn

Shared Journey

She pauses to sniff
  her nose almost touching the ground
  then moves on slowly in search of the next fresh scent
Occasionally she lifts her head, checking to see if I am still there
  and upon finding me, her tail lifts into a reassuring wag
I am not sure at times which of us is in more need of the other
She, who limps with age and cannot hear behind her
  whose eyes have clouded over with time
Needs me to move at her pace on the walks
  to stand patiently as she scours the ground
Or me
  who sometimes rushes from one task to another
  forgetting to breathe, to look around
Who needs her to help me slow my movements
  to stand at the other end of the leash and stretch
Lifting my eyes to follow a crow as it mobs a red tail hawk
  to count the hyacinths ready to bloom
We share sixteen years of memories
We have both aged in our own way
and yet we still move in tandem
A silent bond holding us close

Summary

It is the summer of blue hydrangeas
  and sudden storms
Of clear blue skies
  and gentle breezes
Of muggy mornings where the dew soaks my skin
  as I walk the neighborhood
It is the summer
  of cross eyed baby robins
  squawking as they frantically hop after worm seeking mothers
The summer of weddings
  sparkling eyed brides
  and laughing grooms
It is the summer of ominous dark clouds
  rolling in amidst echoing thunder
  and rain slapping furiously against freshly washed windows
It is the summer of flowers
  tall beyond expectations
  leaning across clover filled lawns
And squirrels digging through freshly potted planters
  looking for last year's acorns
A summer of porch sitting
  and deck drinking
Of Findlay Market tomatoes
  ripe from the sun
And berries bursting with flavor
Of bike rides in the country
  where the sun browns my arms
  and the humidity leaves me dripping
While hawks teach their young to hunt
  and rivers run high and dark from the sumer storms
A summer of days packing and unpacking
Of opening one house and closing another
It is a summer of memory making and destinations still to come

Going East

We traveled East
  leaving the sunset that graced the dogwoods
    with pink shadows each night at nine
  leaving the heat that simmered off concrete pathways
    long before noon
We packed the car and before the sun's earliest rays lit our path
  we traveled East
Dogs sprawled in tandem across the back seat
    their light snore an odd tempo to the radio
We traveled East
    leaving the speeding cars and restaurant malls
    the steamy nights and stuffy days
Through mountain valleys, past fresh vineyards
    and over ancient bridges spanning ship waterways
    haven to osprey nests
We traveled East
    to early sunsets with stars blanketing the endless sky
To even earlier mornings where silence was broken
    by foghorns sounding across the water to wooded acres and
    towering pines
We traveled East

Belfast in August

That sunny afternoon
  the one that seemed much warmer than it was
The one during which our bodies soaked up each shadowed ray
    of light
      after being held captive indoors for three days of rain
with fog so damp the sheets never dried
Then there we were
  sharing a granite boulder on the bay
In the moment you turned to smile
  all joy
  all contentment
I saw you at ten and again at twenty
  Then later at forty or was it fifty
I no longer needed the sun to warm my soul as my heart smiled
  remembering the years behind us
The many threads woven together over time
The simple beauty of the gift of your friendship
  would have brought me through any stretch of rain
And had, so often in the past
So camera in hand, I snapped the photo that later I viewed
And again you were ten, all mischief, all joy
With dreams to chase

Summer Children

Like grounded kites
their bright colors scamper
barefoot throwing up sand
as they bounce and leap
into the waves
dancing and soaring
as kites in the wind
the children of summer

Mom

The tapestry of her life hung in the quiet grief blanketing the air
Its threads fragile
  representing all whose paths she crossed
Years woven together
  by the words of those in the room
Memories they stood to share
Moments encased in hearts already aching
As the absence of her whispered grace
  Became a legacy

I Am

I chased the moon across the fields
  while catching your history in my arms
And let the clouds that hovered near
  erase the memories of yesterday's dawn
I am not the one forgotten
  nor am I the future of the lost
But I am the beacon that will call you home
When your dreams leave you dancing in the wind

Barbara grew up north of Cincinnati in the village of Wyoming. From an early age she enjoyed reading which led to writing poems about the world around her. She was active in a writing group in high school during which she had several poems published. At Wittenberg where she majored in Education, Barbara continued to pursue her writing interests taking numerous extra classes in creative writing. Once out of college, she moved to the countryside and would often use her experiences in Appalachia as topics for short stories and poetry. For the past 31 years, she has sent a personal poem as a Christmas greeting to family and friends. Barbara has participated in numerous writing workshops and classes both in Maine and Cincinnati. In April of 2015, she was one of four winners in the Hamilton Country Library Poetry Contest

Since retiring as a School Social Worker, Barbara has spent her time working with rescue dogs, gardening, kayaking and biking. She enjoys exploring the area around her by bike and has done numerous biking trips abroad. Her outdoor experiences keep her in touch with Nature which is one of her favorite writing topics. She and her husband have two rescue dogs and a cat and divide their time between Maine and Ohio.

www.ingramcontent.com/pod-product-compliance
Lightning Source LLC
LaVergne TN
LVHW021126080426
835510LV00021B/3338